CHER MEMOIR 2024

2024

A Journey Through Fame, Music, and Reinvention

CARL FREEMAN

Disclaimer

This book is an unauthorized and unofficial biography of Cher. It is not affiliated with, endorsed, or authorized by Cher or any of her representatives, agents, or associates. The content within this book is based on publicly available information, interviews, and third-party sources. While every effort has been made to ensure the accuracy of the information presented, the author and publisher do not guarantee the completeness, timeliness, or correctness of the material. All opinions, interpretations, and insights expressed in this biography are those of the author and do not reflect the official views or statements of Cher or her team.

Dedication

To Cher,
For your unwavering strength, boundless talent, and unapologetic authenticity that continue to inspire generations. Your journey is a testament to the power of reinvention, resilience, and the endless pursuit of greatness. This book is a celebration of you—the icon, the artist, the woman—whose story has touched countless lives and whose legacy will live on forever.

And to all those who dare to dream, to stand out, and to never stop evolving. May your courage and spirit guide you as Cher's has guided us.

Table of Contents

Prologue

The Beat Goes On

In an ever-changing world of fleeting fame and transient trends, few stars burn with the brilliance and longevity of Cher. From her first notes in the 1960s as one-half of the iconic Sonny & Cher duo to her reign as a solo sensation and Hollywood icon, Cher's journey has been one of evolution, resilience, and unapologetic authenticity. But why, in 2024, does her story continue to resonate with millions across the globe?

Cher's tale is more than a narrative of fame; it's a testament to the human spirit's boundless capacity for reinvention. In an era where identity is fluid, and success is redefined by each generation, Cher's ability to adapt and thrive across six decades of music, film, and activism serves as a masterclass in perseverance. Her voice, both powerful and vulnerable, transcends the constraints of time and genre, touching hearts and challenging norms with each new chapter.

This memoir explores not just the milestones—the chart-topping hits, the Oscar-winning roles, and the cultural accolades—but the moments of doubt, defiance, and triumph that shaped her journey. Cher's story is one of breaking boundaries, shattering expectations, and creating a legacy that defies convention.

As we look back through the lens of 2024, a time marked by rapid societal shifts and a quest for authenticity, Cher's life offers a blueprint for navigating change without losing oneself. She remains a beacon of courage, creativity, and conviction—a symbol of what it means to stay true to one's essence while embracing the new.

The beat goes on, and so does Cher. This is her story.

Chapter 1

Humble Beginnings

Long before she became known to the world simply as Cher, she was Cherilyn Sarkisian, born on May 20, 1946, in the small town of El Centro, California. Her story began under the sun-drenched skies of Southern California, far from the glitz and glamour she would one day command. The daughter of an Armenian-American truck driver and a mother with a flair for acting and modeling, Cher's early life was a complex tapestry of dreams, struggles, and determination.

Raised by her mother, Georgia Holt, who often juggled multiple jobs to make ends meet, Cher's childhood was marked by financial instability but rich in imagination and resilience. Georgia's passion for the arts was a formative influence, often filling their modest home with music and aspirations of a better life. From an early age, Cherilyn displayed a spark—a confidence that belied her years and a voice that carried a hint of the power it would one day wield.

A Nomadic Youth

Cher's early years were anything but stable. Her family moved frequently, often in search of better opportunities, and she attended numerous schools, which made it difficult for her to establish roots. This nomadic lifestyle could have been destabilizing, but for Cher, it was formative. Each move brought new challenges, new friends, and new experiences that would shape her adaptability—a trait that would become her hallmark in her later career.

Despite the financial hardships, her mother nurtured her artistic inclinations. Georgia often took Cher to the movies, and it was in those darkened theaters that the young girl first fell in love with the idea of performing. Watching stars like Audrey Hepburn and Bette Davis, Cherilyn began to dream of a future where she, too, could command the screen. However, she wasn't just drawn to acting; music held a special allure. The records playing on the radio sparked a fire in her heart, and she began to imitate the singers she admired.

Discovering Her Voice

Cherilyn's voice was unique even then. Deep, resonant, and filled with emotion, it set her apart from the other girls in her school. She joined choirs and performed in school productions, but it wasn't until her teenage years that she began to seriously consider a career in music. By the time she was 16, she had dropped out of high school to pursue her dreams full-time. It was a bold move, but one that spoke to her determination.

In the early 1960s, Cherilyn moved to Los Angeles, a city pulsating with the promise of fame and fortune. It was here, in the bustling heart of the entertainment industry, that she would take her first steps toward becoming the icon we know today. She found work as a backup singer, navigating the competitive world of the music industry with a mixture of naivety and grit. During this time, she met Salvatore "Sonny" Bono, a meeting that would change the course of her life.

The Turning Point: Meeting Sonny
Sonny Bono was working for legendary producer Phil Spector, and he saw something in Cherilyn that others had overlooked. Their partnership began professionally, but it quickly evolved into a personal and creative bond that would catapult them both to fame. Sonny believed in Cher's talent, and together, they began to carve out a space in the music industry. He introduced her to Spector, and

she recorded background vocals on some of his tracks, including the iconic "Be My Baby" by The Ronettes.

It wasn't long before Sonny and Cher decided to strike out on their own. They formed a duo, initially performing under the name Caesar and Cleo before rebranding as Sonny & Cher. Their breakthrough came with the release of "I Got You Babe" in 1965—a song that captured the spirit of the era and established them as one of the most beloved acts of the 1960s.

Resilience in Adversity

The journey from Cherilyn Sarkisian to Cher wasn't an easy one. She faced rejection, skepticism, and the constant pressure to conform. In an industry dominated by men and defined by rigid expectations, Cher's unapologetic individuality set her apart but also made her a target. She refused to be boxed in, embracing her heritage, her distinctive voice, and her unconventional style.

Her early experiences—moving from town to town, watching her mother struggle to make ends meet, dropping out of school to chase a seemingly impossible dream—instilled in her a resilience that would serve her well throughout her career. She learned early on that success wasn't guaranteed, but it was worth fighting for.

A Star in the Making

As the 1960s drew to a close, Cher was on the brink of stardom. The foundation had been laid in those humble beginnings, in the small towns and modest homes where she first dreamed of something more. Her journey was just beginning, but the lessons she learned during those formative years would stay with her. They would shape her music, her acting, and her approach to life.

Cherilyn Sarkisian had become Cher—a name that would soon become synonymous with strength, reinvention, and enduring talent. Her story was only beginning, but even in those early years, the seeds of greatness had been sown.

Chapter 2

Sonny & Cher—Rise of a Power Duo

In the bustling music scene of 1960s Los Angeles, two seemingly unlikely individuals crossed paths, setting the stage for one of the most iconic duos in pop history. When Cherilyn Sarkisian met Salvatore "Sonny" Bono, neither could have predicted the profound impact their partnership would have on music, culture, and their personal lives. Their journey was one of serendipity, ambition, and an undeniable chemistry that transcended their differences and defined an era.

A Fateful Encounter

Cher and Sonny first met in 1962. At the time, Cher was just 16 and navigating the gritty music industry while Sonny, 11 years her senior, was working for the influential producer Phil Spector. Sonny's outgoing personality and industry experience contrasted sharply with Cher's quiet determination, but they shared an ambition that would soon intertwine their fates. Sonny saw a spark in Cher—a raw talent and magnetism that set her apart from others. For Cher, Sonny represented a guiding force in a daunting industry, a mentor who believed in her potential even when others didn't.

Their relationship quickly evolved from a professional collaboration into something deeply personal. They moved in together, with Cher taking on household responsibilities and Sonny helping her hone her craft. This unconventional dynamic formed the foundation of a powerful creative partnership. Sonny taught Cher about the intricacies of the music industry, while Cher inspired Sonny with her distinctive voice and evolving stage presence.

Early Struggles and First Steps
Their initial foray into the music scene was anything but glamorous. They started performing as "Caesar and Cleo," a name that reflected Sonny's fascination with history but failed to capture the public's imagination. Their early singles, while showing promise, didn't gain much traction. The duo faced repeated rejection and financial struggles, but they remained undeterred. They believed in their potential and were willing to put in the work.

Their breakthrough came not with a hit song but through relentless perseverance and experimentation. Sonny's knack for songwriting and production, combined with Cher's distinctive contralto voice, gradually began to catch the attention of audiences. They refined their sound, blending folk-rock with pop sensibilities, and adopted a new moniker: Sonny & Cher.

The Birth of "I Got You Babe"
In 1965, their fortunes changed with the release of "I Got You Babe." Written by Sonny, the song was an anthem of young love, perfectly capturing the optimism and countercultural spirit of the 1960s. Its simple yet heartfelt lyrics, combined with the duo's undeniable chemistry, struck a chord with listeners. The song topped the Billboard Hot 100 and became an instant classic.

"I Got You Babe" wasn't just a commercial success; it was a cultural phenomenon. The duo's image—Sonny's bohemian style and Cher's exotic beauty—resonated with the emerging youth movement. They were different, authentic, and unapologetically themselves, which made them icons of the era. The song's success catapulted them into the limelight, transforming them from struggling artists into household names.

Crafting Their Identity

What set Sonny & Cher apart was their unique dynamic. Sonny was the creative mastermind and producer, while Cher was the captivating performer with a voice that could convey both vulnerability and strength. Together, they created a sound and image that defied convention. They weren't just musical partners; they were a brand, a concept that was both romantic and rebellious.

Their subsequent hits, including "The Beat Goes On" and "Baby Don't Go," reinforced their status as pop stars. Each song reflected their evolving style, blending folk, rock, and pop in ways that felt fresh and innovative. Their music wasn't just about catchy melodies; it carried messages of love, resilience, and social commentary that resonated with the turbulent 1960s.

Television Stardom: The Sonny & Cher Comedy Hour

As their music career soared, Sonny & Cher expanded their influence beyond the recording studio. In 1971, they launched "The Sonny & Cher Comedy Hour," a variety show that showcased their musical talents, comedic skits, and undeniable chemistry. The show was a massive success, drawing millions of viewers and solidifying their status as cultural icons. Cher's glamorous outfits and sharp wit, combined with Sonny's self-deprecating humor, made them a beloved television duo.

The show's success marked a turning point in their careers. It wasn't just about music anymore; they had become multifaceted entertainers, with a platform that reached a broad audience. Cher, in particular, began to emerge as a star in her own right. Her fashion choices, bold personality, and magnetic presence made her a trendsetter and role model for women.

Behind the Scenes: Personal Dynamics and Challenges

While their public image was one of harmony and partnership, behind the scenes, their relationship was complex. Sonny was the dominant force in their creative and business dealings, often making decisions without consulting Cher. This dynamic, while successful professionally, created tension in their personal lives. Cher's growing independence and desire for creative control clashed with Sonny's vision, leading to conflicts that would ultimately strain their relationship.

Despite these challenges, their partnership endured for years, driven by a shared history and mutual respect. They navigated the highs and lows of fame together, weathering controversies, financial struggles, and the pressures of the spotlight. However, by the mid-1970s, cracks began to appear in their relationship. Cher's rising star and evolving ambitions made it increasingly difficult to maintain the partnership that had defined their careers.

The Legacy of Sonny & Cher
Sonny & Cher's rise to fame was more than a story of musical success; it was a testament to the power of partnership and perseverance. They defied the odds, creating a legacy that would outlast their personal and professional relationship. Their music, television show, and cultural impact laid the groundwork for Cher's future as a solo artist and global icon.

As the 1960s gave way to the 1970s, the world was changing, and so were Sonny and Cher. Their journey together had reached its peak, but their story was far from over. For Cher, the end of Sonny & Cher was just the beginning of a new chapter—one that would see her rise to even greater heights as a solo artist and actress.

Chapter 3

Breaking the Mold

As the curtain fell on Sonny & Cher's golden era, Cher found herself standing at a crossroads. No longer part of a duo, she faced the daunting task of carving out a solo identity in an industry that had long defined her as half of an inseparable pair. The world knew her as the sultry-voiced, exotic half of Sonny & Cher, but Cher had always harbored ambitions that extended beyond the confines of their partnership. She was determined to break free from the image that had both catapulted her to fame and confined her to a specific role. This was not just a reinvention; it was a reclamation.

Stepping Out of the Shadows

The dissolution of Sonny & Cher's marriage in 1974 was not merely the end of a personal relationship; it marked the beginning of a profound professional transformation. For Cher, the separation was a painful yet liberating experience. While Sonny had been her mentor and partner, his dominance in their creative process often left her feeling stifled.

Now, she had the opportunity to step into the spotlight on her own terms.

Her first attempts at a solo career had already begun while still with Sonny, but they had largely been side projects. Now, she was ready to fully embrace the challenge. Her first major solo hit came with "Gypsys, Tramps & Thieves" in 1971, followed by "Half-Breed" and "Dark Lady," songs that showcased not only her vocal range but also her willingness to tackle controversial themes. These tracks told stories of marginalized people, reflecting Cher's deep empathy and desire to give a voice to the voiceless. Each song reached the top of the Billboard charts, proving that she could succeed outside the shadow of Sonny.

Confronting Industry Bias

Despite her early solo successes, Cher faced significant obstacles. The music industry, still largely male-dominated, often viewed female artists through a narrow lens. Cher's distinctive contralto voice, striking appearance, and bold persona made her a target for both adoration and criticism. Many industry executives dismissed her as a mere pop culture phenomenon, failing to see the depth of her artistry. But Cher had never been one to shy away from a challenge.

Determined to prove her versatility, she took on a range of musical styles, from rock to disco. Each genre shift was met with skepticism, but Cher saw these transitions as opportunities for growth. Her 1975 album *Stars* showcased her willingness to experiment, blending elements of rock and pop. Though it wasn't a commercial success, it marked an important step in her evolution as an artist. She was no longer content to be boxed into a single category.

The Vegas Chapter

In the mid-1970s, as her music career faced ups and downs, Cher found a new platform: Las Vegas. She launched a residency that became an instant sensation. Her elaborate costumes, dramatic performances, and powerhouse vocals drew audiences from around the world. Vegas became a proving ground, a place where she could experiment with her image and performance style. It was here that Cher honed the theatricality that would become a hallmark of her later tours.

The Vegas shows were not just concerts; they were spectacles. Cher's ability to reinvent herself with each performance kept audiences captivated. She wasn't just singing; she was telling stories, creating characters, and pushing the boundaries of what a live performance could be. This period was crucial in solidifying her reputation as an entertainer who defied conventions.

Reinvention Through Acting

Even as she battled industry biases in music, Cher began to explore another avenue: acting. Hollywood had long been an interest, but the transition from music to film was fraught with challenges. Many doubted her ability to succeed as an actress, dismissing her as a singer trying to capitalize on her fame. Cher, however, was determined to prove them wrong.

Her breakthrough came with a role in *Silkwood* (1983), where she starred alongside Meryl Streep. Playing a lesbian factory worker, Cher delivered a performance that was both raw and nuanced, earning her an Academy Award nomination for Best Supporting Actress. Critics who had once doubted her acting chops were forced to reconsider. This was a turning point; Cher had proven that she was more than just a pop star—she was a serious actress.

This success opened the door to more film roles. In *Mask* (1985), she portrayed the mother of a disfigured boy, earning critical acclaim for her powerful performance. But it was *Moonstruck* (1987) that cemented her status as a Hollywood star. Her portrayal of Loretta Castorini, a widowed Italian-American woman, won her the Academy Award for Best Actress. Cher had not only broken the mold; she had shattered it.

Facing the Critics and Redefining Success
Throughout her solo career, Cher faced relentless scrutiny. Critics often dismissed her bold fashion choices and theatrical performances, failing to see the artistry behind them. But Cher refused to conform. She embraced her uniqueness, using fashion as a form of self-expression and a way to challenge societal norms. Her iconic outfits—designed by Bob Mackie—became symbols of her defiance and creativity.

Cher's willingness to take risks, both musically and personally, was a key factor in her success. She wasn't afraid to fail, and each setback only fueled her determination. She understood that breaking the mold meant enduring criticism, but she also knew that true success lay in authenticity.

The Legacy of Reinvention

By the late 1980s, Cher had established herself as a multifaceted artist. She had conquered music, television, and film, defying expectations at every turn. Her journey was a testament to the power of reinvention and resilience. She had broken free from the image that had defined her early career, emerging as a symbol of strength and independence.

Cher's solo career was not just about achieving success; it was about redefining what success looked like. She had faced rejection, industry bias, and personal challenges, but she had never compromised her vision. Her story was one of courage, creativity, and an unyielding belief in herself.

As the 1990s approached, Cher's career was far from over. In fact, some of her most iconic moments were still to come. She had broken the mold, but she wasn't done yet. The world would soon see that for Cher, reinvention wasn't just a career strategy—it was a way of life.

Chapter 4

Hollywood Dreams

Cher's journey into acting was not an inevitable extension of her fame in music. For many in the entertainment industry, the transition from pop star to respected actress was a treacherous path littered with skepticism and doubt. The glamorous spotlight of Hollywood had a way of harshly exposing anyone it deemed unworthy. Yet, for Cher, it was a calling—an opportunity to prove that she was more than a chart-topping singer with a magnetic stage presence. Her foray into acting was not about seeking validation but rather a natural progression in her quest for artistic fulfillment. It would be a battle against typecasting, industry prejudice, and her own self-doubt. Ultimately, it would culminate in triumphs that even her harshest critics could not ignore.

Early Steps on a New Stage

Cher's first exposure to acting came during her time on *The Sonny & Cher Comedy Hour*. The variety show included comedic sketches that showcased her natural flair for performance. While she initially viewed these segments as light-hearted fun, they revealed a hidden talent. Cher possessed an innate ability to inhabit characters, using her expressive face and dynamic presence to captivate audiences. But comedy skits were one thing; Hollywood was another beast entirely.

Her first major film role came in 1967 with *Good Times*, directed by William Friedkin. The film, a surreal musical comedy co-starring Sonny Bono, failed to make an impact, both critically and commercially. While it showcased the duo's charisma, it did little to establish Cher as a serious actress. This initial stumble reinforced the industry's perception that musicians had no place in Hollywood. For Cher, it was a humbling experience, but it also ignited a determination to return to the screen on her own terms.

Throughout the 1970s, Cher's acting ambitions took a backseat to her music career and television commitments. However, the desire to prove herself as an actress never waned. She knew that to be taken seriously, she would need a role that challenged her, something far removed from the glitz and glamor that had defined her public persona.

A Breakthrough with *Silkwood*

The turning point came in the early 1980s
when Cher was cast in *Silkwood* (1983).
Directed by Mike Nichols and starring Meryl
Streep and Kurt Russell, the film was a gritty
drama based on the true story of Karen
Silkwood, a whistleblower at a nuclear facility.
Cher played Dolly Pelliker, Karen's roommate
and confidante, a role that required her to
shed the glamorous image she had cultivated
for years. Dolly was a working-class woman,
rough around the edges, a stark departure
from the fashion icon the world knew.

Cher's preparation for the role was intense.
She immersed herself in the character,
studying the nuances of working-class life and
exploring the depths of human vulnerability.
On set, she was surrounded by seasoned
actors, including Streep, whose dedication set
a high bar. Cher was determined not to be
outshined. She worked tirelessly, seeking
advice from Nichols and her co-stars,
determined to deliver a performance that
would silence her critics.

The result was transformative. Cher's
portrayal of Dolly was raw, authentic, and

emotionally resonant. Critics who had once dismissed her were now forced to acknowledge her talent. The performance earned her a Golden Globe nomination and, more importantly, respect from the acting community. For Cher, *Silkwood* was more than just a film; it was a validation of her potential as an actress.

Proving Her Mettle: *Mask* and *Moonstruck*

Following *Silkwood*, Cher was no longer viewed as a musician dabbling in acting. She had proven she could hold her own on screen. Her next significant role came in *Mask* (1985), directed by Peter Bogdanovich. Cher played Rusty Dennis, the tough, loving mother of a boy with a severe facial deformity. The role was emotionally demanding, requiring Cher to tap into deep reservoirs of empathy and strength. Rusty was a complex character— flawed yet fiercely protective of her son.

Cher's performance in *Mask* was nothing short of riveting. She portrayed Rusty with a raw intensity that resonated deeply with audiences. The role earned her the Best Actress award at the Cannes Film Festival and further solidified her reputation as a serious actress. Critics praised her ability to convey both the vulnerability and strength of a mother fighting for her son's dignity. It was a role that showcased the full range of her talent and laid the groundwork for her most iconic performance yet.

In 1987, Cher took on the role of Loretta Castorini in *Moonstruck*, a romantic comedy directed by Norman Jewison. Playing a widowed Italian-American woman caught in a whirlwind romance, Cher delivered a performance that was both heartfelt and comedic. Loretta was a character full of contradictions—pragmatic yet romantic, cautious yet passionate. Cher's portrayal captured these nuances with a brilliance that few had anticipated.

Moonstruck was a critical and commercial success. Cher's performance was universally lauded, and she received the Academy Award for Best Actress. In her acceptance speech, she acknowledged the doubts and obstacles she had faced, expressing gratitude to those who had believed in her. Winning the Oscar was not just a personal victory; it was a culmination of years of perseverance and a definitive rebuttal to those who had underestimated her.

A New Era of Respect

With her Oscar win, Cher had achieved what few could: she had successfully transitioned from pop star to acclaimed actress. Hollywood, once skeptical of her ambitions, now recognized her as a formidable talent. She continued to take on diverse roles, refusing to be pigeonholed. Each performance was a testament to her versatility and commitment to her craft.

Cher's journey in Hollywood was not just about achieving success; it was about breaking barriers and redefining what was possible. She had faced prejudice, endured rejection, and defied expectations, emerging stronger each time. Her story was one of resilience, courage, and an unyielding belief in her own potential.

As the 1990s dawned, Cher's Hollywood dreams had not only been realized—they had become an integral part of her legacy. She had proven that true artistry knows no boundaries, and that reinvention is not just a career strategy but a way of life.

Chapter 5

Reinvention and Resilience

Few artists in the history of entertainment have demonstrated the ability to reinvent themselves as masterfully as Cher. Across decades and genres, she has seamlessly navigated the shifting tides of the music industry, emerging not just relevant but dominant in each era. From her early days as a pop-folk icon with Sonny & Cher to becoming a solo sensation, disco diva, rock goddess, and dance-pop queen, Cher's journey is a testament to resilience, creativity, and an unparalleled understanding of cultural evolution. Reinvention, for Cher, is not merely a survival strategy—it is an art form.

The 1970s: Disco Awakening

By the late 1970s, the world of music had shifted. Rock's dominance was being challenged by a new cultural force: disco. Characterized by its infectious beats, lush orchestration, and hedonistic spirit, disco was more than just a genre—it was a movement. For Cher, it presented both an opportunity and a challenge. She had already proven her versatility, but the transition to disco required more than just a change in sound; it demanded a transformation in persona.

Her foray into disco began with the album *Take Me Home* (1979). The title track, a pulsating anthem with a hypnotic beat, became an instant hit. Cher embraced the genre with gusto, donning glittering costumes and immersing herself in the era's flamboyant aesthetic. The song reached the Top 10 on the Billboard Hot 100, marking a successful reinvention. *Take Me Home* wasn't just a commercial triumph; it was a declaration of Cher's ability to adapt and thrive in a rapidly changing musical landscape.

However, the disco era was short-lived. By the early 1980s, the backlash against disco was in full swing, and Cher found herself at another crossroads. Rather than clinging to a fading trend, she set her sights on a new challenge: rock.

The 1980s: Embracing Rock's Raw Power

The 1980s marked a turning point in Cher's career. With disco fading, she needed to once again redefine herself. This time, she turned to rock—a genre that was experiencing a resurgence. Rock was raw, rebellious, and powerful, qualities that resonated deeply with Cher. It was also a chance to showcase a different side of herself: one that was fierce, unapologetic, and deeply authentic.

Her return to the charts came with the album *I Paralyze* (1982), a blend of rock and new wave influences. While the album didn't achieve significant commercial success, it laid the groundwork for what was to come. Cher's rock persona would fully crystallize with her next albums, *Cher* (1987) and *Heart of Stone* (1989). These records marked a definitive shift, featuring gritty vocals, anthemic choruses, and collaborations with some of the biggest names in rock.

Songs like "I Found Someone," "If I Could Turn Back Time," and "Just Like Jesse James" became instant classics. "If I Could Turn Back Time," in particular, became iconic—not just for its powerful lyrics and soaring melody but for its controversial music video, which featured Cher in a sheer bodysuit, straddling a cannon on a naval ship. The video sparked outrage and fascination in equal measure, further cementing Cher's reputation as a boundary-pusher.

Her foray into rock wasn't just a stylistic choice; it was a statement. In a genre often dominated by male voices, Cher carved out a space for herself, proving that she could hold her own with the best of them. The rock era also highlighted her resilience. Each song, each performance, was infused with a sense of defiance and survival. She wasn't just singing about heartbreak and redemption; she was living it.

The 1990s: The Dance-Pop Renaissance

As the 1990s dawned, music was once again in flux. Grunge and hip-hop were on the rise, and the industry was undergoing a digital revolution. For many artists of Cher's generation, this period marked a decline. But Cher saw it as another opportunity for reinvention. She turned her attention to dance music, a genre that was gaining popularity in clubs around the world.

Her 1998 album, *Believe*, was a game-changer. The title track, with its infectious beat and pioneering use of Auto-Tune, became a global phenomenon. The song's distinctive vocal effect, which came to be known as the "Cher effect," was groundbreaking. At a time when many artists were resistant to digital technology, Cher embraced it, using Auto-Tune not to mask imperfections but as a creative tool. "Believe" topped charts in over 20 countries and became one of the best-selling singles of all time.

The success of *Believe* was more than just a commercial victory; it was a cultural moment. Cher had once again proven that she could not only adapt to changing trends but also shape them. The dance-pop era of the late 1990s and early 2000s saw Cher at the height of her powers, connecting with a new generation of fans while staying true to her core identity.

The 2000s and Beyond: A Legacy of Reinvention

As the 21st century unfolded, Cher continued to evolve. She launched a highly successful Las Vegas residency, *Cher at the Colosseum*, which ran from 2008 to 2011. The show was a testament to her enduring appeal, featuring elaborate sets, stunning costumes, and a career-spanning setlist. Each performance was a reminder of Cher's ability to reinvent herself, not just musically but visually and theatrically.

In 2013, she released *Closer to the Truth*, an album that blended pop, dance, and rock influences. Tracks like "Woman's World" and "I Hope You Find It" showcased her versatility and willingness to experiment. Even in her 60s, Cher was pushing boundaries and exploring new creative avenues.

Her resilience extended beyond music. In 2018, she returned to the big screen with a scene-stealing role in *Mamma Mia! Here We Go Again*, proving that her charisma and talent remained undiminished. The film introduced Cher to yet another generation, reinforcing her status as a timeless icon.

The Art of Reinvention

Cher's ability to reinvent herself is not just a career strategy; it's a reflection of her resilience and authenticity. Each transformation has been a response to the times, but also a reflection of her inner journey. She has never been content to rest on past successes or conform to expectations. Instead, she has continually pushed herself, embracing change with courage and creativity.

Her story is a reminder that true resilience is not just about surviving—it's about thriving, evolving, and staying true to oneself. In an industry known for its fickleness, Cher has remained a constant, not by staying the same, but by daring to be different.

Chapter 6

The Comeback Queen

Cher's enduring career is not just a story of longevity; it's a saga of comebacks—each more dazzling and triumphant than the last. Unlike many artists who fade with time, Cher has a knack for rising from perceived career lows, re-emerging with groundbreaking albums, electrifying tours, and cultural moments that leave a lasting impact. Her resilience and determination have earned her the well-deserved title of "The Comeback Queen," a moniker that underscores her unmatched ability to reinvent herself and reclaim the spotlight. From the revolutionary *Believe* era to her record-breaking Las Vegas residency, each comeback not only revitalized her career but redefined her legacy.

The Road to "Believe"

By the mid-1990s, Cher's career had hit a plateau. While she was respected as an actress and a music legend, the music industry was evolving rapidly. Grunge, hip-hop, and teen pop dominated the charts, and many saw Cher as part of an earlier era.

Some critics speculated that her time as a chart-topping artist had passed. However, Cher, with her signature tenacity, saw this as an opportunity to reassert her relevance.

In 1998, she began working on what would become *Believe*. Initially, there was skepticism—could an artist known for rock anthems and ballads adapt to the emerging electronic dance music (EDM) scene? Cher not only adapted; she transformed the genre. The album's title track, "Believe," became a cultural phenomenon. Its use of Auto-Tune—a relatively new technology at the time—was groundbreaking. Rather than using it to correct pitch, Cher and her producers applied it creatively, producing a robotic, ethereal effect that became the song's signature.

"Believe" was more than just a chart-topping hit; it was a statement of defiance and empowerment. The lyrics, with their themes of resilience and self-reliance, resonated deeply with listeners. The song topped charts in over 20 countries, sold millions of copies, and won a Grammy for Best Dance Recording. It marked the beginning of a new era for Cher, proving that she could not only keep up with the times but set the pace. The success of *Believe* catapulted her back to the forefront of pop music, reintroducing her to a new generation of fans.

The "Do You Believe?" Tour

With the success of *Believe*, Cher embarked on one of her most ambitious tours to date: the *Do You Believe? Tour* (1999-2000). Spanning North America, Europe, and Australia, the tour was a spectacular showcase of her musical evolution. Each performance was a high-energy blend of her greatest hits, new dance anthems, and elaborate visual productions. Cher, at 53, defied industry norms, proving that age was no barrier to delivering electrifying performances.

The tour was a critical and commercial success, grossing over $70 million—a testament to Cher's enduring appeal. Fans were treated to a theatrical experience, complete with elaborate costumes, intricate choreography, and state-of-the-art special effects. Each show was a celebration of Cher's journey, highlighting her ability to stay ahead of trends while honoring her roots.

Living Proof and the Farewell Tour

Following the success of *Believe*, Cher released *Living Proof* in 2001, another dance-pop album that featured hits like "Song for the Lonely." While the album didn't match the meteoric success of *Believe*, it reinforced Cher's dominance in the dance genre. However, it was the accompanying tour, the *Living Proof: The Farewell Tour* (2002-2005), that truly cemented her status as the ultimate comeback queen.

Originally conceived as a final farewell to touring, the tour became one of the most successful in history, grossing over $250 million. It was a spectacle of epic proportions, featuring over-the-top costumes, stunning visual effects, and a setlist that spanned Cher's entire career. Each performance was a retrospective, a journey through the decades that highlighted her evolution as an artist. The farewell tour was anything but somber; it was a triumphant celebration of resilience and reinvention.

Cher's announcement that it would be her final tour added an emotional weight to each performance. Fans flocked to see her, knowing it might be their last chance to witness her magic on stage. However, true to her nature, Cher would soon return, defying expectations once again.

Las Vegas: Reinventing the Residency

In 2008, Cher launched *Cher at the Colosseum*, a residency at Caesars Palace in Las Vegas. At the time, Las Vegas residencies were often seen as career endpoints—comfortable gigs for artists past their prime. Cher, however, transformed the residency into a cultural event, setting a new standard for what a Las Vegas show could be.

The residency ran from 2008 to 2011 and featured over 200 performances. Each show was a dazzling display of Cher's artistry, featuring elaborate sets, stunning costumes designed by Bob Mackie, and a setlist that spanned her entire career. The production was a testament to her versatility, blending pop, rock, and dance with theatrical flair. Audiences were treated to a multi-sensory experience that highlighted Cher's evolution as an artist.

The success of her residency paved the way for other pop stars, including Britney Spears, Lady Gaga, and Celine Dion, to follow suit. Cher had once again redefined the rules, turning a Las Vegas residency into a prestigious, career-revitalizing endeavor.

"Here We Go Again" and the Legacy of Resilience

In 2018, Cher embarked on the *Here We Go Again Tour*, following her appearance in *Mamma Mia! Here We Go Again*. The tour was a global success, grossing over $112 million. At 72, Cher proved that her energy, charisma, and voice remained undiminished. Each performance was a testament to her resilience, a reminder that true artistry knows no age.

The tour's setlist spanned her entire career, from her early hits with Sonny Bono to her latest dance anthems. It was a celebration of survival and reinvention, a journey through the decades that highlighted Cher's unparalleled ability to adapt and thrive.

The Essence of the Comeback Queen

Cher's story is one of resilience, creativity, and an unyielding determination to defy expectations. Each comeback has been more than just a return to the spotlight; it has been a reinvention, a redefinition of what it means to be an artist. Cher has never been content to rest on past successes. Instead, she has continually pushed herself, embracing change with courage and creativity. Her comebacks are not just triumphs of talent—they are triumphs of spirit.

Chapter 7

Behind the Curtain

Behind the dazzling performances, iconic fashion, and chart-topping hits lies a deeply personal story of love, loss, triumph, and vulnerability. Cher's public persona is larger than life, but her private journey—marked by marriages, motherhood, and personal challenges—reveals the woman behind the icon. Through decades of scrutiny and adoration, she has navigated her personal life with the same resilience and determination that define her career. This chapter peels back the layers to explore the intimate facets of Cher's life, offering a glimpse into the relationships and experiences that shaped her.

Love and Loss: The Marriages

Cher's romantic life has been a topic of public fascination since the 1960s. Her high-profile relationships, particularly her marriages to Sonny Bono and Gregg Allman, were not just tabloid fodder—they were integral chapters in her journey of self-discovery and growth.

Sonny Bono: The Partner and the Paradox

Cher's relationship with Sonny Bono is perhaps the most well-documented and complex of her life. They met in 1962 when Cher was just 16 and Sonny was 27. Their connection was immediate, and their partnership quickly evolved from a personal relationship into a professional collaboration that would define an era.

Their marriage, which began in 1964, was marked by intense highs and lows. Together, they created a brand that was both magnetic and tumultuous. The duo's public image was that of a harmonious couple, but behind the scenes, the dynamics were far more complicated. Cher often spoke of Sonny's controlling nature, acknowledging that while he was instrumental in her early success, their relationship was fraught with challenges. Despite the difficulties, Sonny's influence on Cher's life was profound.

Their divorce in 1975 marked the end of an era. Cher's decision to part ways was a bold move, symbolizing her desire for independence both personally and professionally. In the years following their split, Cher and Sonny maintained a complicated relationship, marked by periods of estrangement and reconciliation. Sonny's tragic death in a skiing accident in 1998 was a turning point for Cher, prompting her to reflect on their shared history. Her eulogy at his funeral was heartfelt, a poignant tribute to the man who had been her partner, mentor, and, in many ways, her adversary.

Gregg Allman: The Rock Star Romance
Cher's second marriage to Gregg Allman, the legendary musician from the Allman Brothers Band, was a stark contrast to her relationship with Sonny. They married in 1975, just days after her divorce from Sonny was finalized. Their relationship was passionate but turbulent, marked by Allman's struggles with substance abuse.

Cher often described their marriage as a whirlwind. They had a deep emotional connection, but the challenges of addiction and the pressures of fame took their toll. They had one son together, Elijah Blue Allman, born in 1976. Cher's decision to end the marriage in 1979 was a difficult but necessary one. Despite their differences, Cher and Gregg remained connected, and she has often spoken about the love and respect she still holds for him.

Motherhood: The Heart of Her World

For Cher, motherhood has been one of the most profound and challenging aspects of her life. She has two children: Chaz Bono, born Chastity Bono, from her marriage to Sonny, and Elijah Blue Allman from her marriage to Gregg Allman.

Chaz Bono: A Journey of Identity and Acceptance

Cher's relationship with Chaz has been a deeply personal and, at times, public journey. Chaz came out as a lesbian in 1995 and later transitioned to male, undergoing gender confirmation surgery in 2009. Cher's initial reaction to Chaz's coming out was mixed, and she has openly admitted to struggling with acceptance. However, over time, Cher became one of Chaz's most vocal supporters, using her platform to advocate for LGBTQ+ rights.

Their relationship is a testament to the evolving nature of parental love. Cher's journey with Chaz has been one of learning, growth, and unconditional love. She has often spoken about how Chaz's courage and authenticity have inspired her. Their bond, while complex, is rooted in a deep mutual respect and understanding.

Elijah Blue Allman: Navigating the Shadows of Fame

Cher's relationship with Elijah Blue has been marked by periods of estrangement and reconciliation. As the child of two famous parents, Elijah struggled with the pressures of living in the public eye. He has battled addiction and has often spoken about the challenges of growing up with a larger-than-life mother.

Cher's love for Elijah is unwavering, and their relationship has evolved over the years. She has been candid about the difficulties of balancing her career with motherhood, acknowledging that her fame often created challenges for her children. Despite the obstacles, Cher's commitment to her family remains a central aspect of her identity.

Personal Struggles: Health and Loss

Cher's journey has not been without its personal struggles. She has faced health challenges, including a long battle with chronic fatigue syndrome, which she was diagnosed with in the 1990s. The condition left her bedridden for months, and she has often spoken about the toll it took on her physically and emotionally.

Beyond health issues, Cher has experienced profound losses. The deaths of Sonny Bono and Gregg Allman were significant blows, and she has also mourned the loss of close friends and family members. Each loss has left its mark, but Cher's ability to process grief and transform it into strength is a testament to her resilience.

The Woman Behind the Icon

Cher's personal life is a mosaic of triumphs and challenges. Her marriages, her experiences as a mother, and her personal struggles have shaped the woman behind the icon. Through it all, she has remained true to herself, navigating the complexities of fame, love, and loss with grace and tenacity.

Her story is not just one of success; it's a story of survival. Cher's ability to confront adversity head-on, to learn from her experiences, and to emerge stronger is what truly defines her. Behind the curtain of glitter and glamour lies a woman of extraordinary depth, a testament to the power of resilience and authenticity.

Chapter 8

Activism and Philanthropy

Cher's legacy extends far beyond the realms of music, film, and fashion. While the public often sees her as an entertainer, her impact on the world is equally profound in the areas of activism and philanthropy. With her characteristic fearlessness, Cher has consistently leveraged her platform to advocate for causes close to her heart, from LGBTQ+ rights and humanitarian crises to political activism. Her unwavering commitment to justice and equality underscores a deep-seated belief in using fame as a tool for positive change. This chapter explores the multifaceted dimensions of Cher's activism and the enduring impact of her philanthropic endeavors.

Advocacy for LGBTQ+ Rights: A Personal and Public Mission

Cher's advocacy for the LGBTQ+ community is perhaps one of the most personal facets of her activism. Her journey into LGBTQ+ advocacy began long before it became a mainstream cause, fueled initially by her close connections with friends and colleagues in the entertainment industry. However, it was her relationship with her child, Chaz Bono, that transformed her activism into a deeply personal mission.

A Mother's Journey

When Chaz came out as a lesbian in 1995, Cher's reaction was mixed. She has openly admitted to struggling with acceptance initially, reflecting the societal attitudes of the time. However, her love for Chaz ultimately guided her toward understanding and advocacy. When Chaz transitioned in 2009, Cher faced another emotional and educational journey. Her candid discussions about this process have resonated with countless families navigating similar experiences.

Cher became one of the most high-profile supporters of transgender rights, using her platform to challenge misconceptions and promote acceptance. She has consistently spoken out against discrimination, emphasizing the importance of love, understanding, and education. Her journey with Chaz has not only strengthened their bond but has also made Cher a powerful voice for the LGBTQ+ community.

Public Advocacy and Influence

Beyond her personal journey, Cher has been an outspoken advocate for LGBTQ+ rights on a broader scale. She has participated in numerous Pride events, spoken at rallies, and used social media to amplify important issues. In 2013, she made headlines when she declined an invitation to perform at the Winter Olympics in Sochi, Russia, citing the country's oppressive anti-LGBTQ+ laws. Her decision was a bold statement, reflecting her commitment to standing against injustice, regardless of the personal or professional cost.

Cher's advocacy has had a tangible impact, inspiring countless individuals and contributing to a broader cultural shift toward acceptance and equality. Her voice has been instrumental in challenging stereotypes, promoting visibility, and fostering a more inclusive society.

Humanitarian Work: Compassion in Action

Cher's humanitarian efforts extend far beyond LGBTQ+ advocacy. She has consistently demonstrated a deep commitment to humanitarian causes, often stepping in where others hesitate. Her work spans a wide range of issues, from disaster relief and refugee support to animal welfare and veterans' rights.

Crisis Response and Relief Efforts

Cher has been at the forefront of numerous disaster relief efforts, often donating significant sums of money and raising awareness through her public platform. After the devastating earthquake in Haiti in 2010, she contributed to relief efforts and encouraged her fans to do the same. Similarly, in the aftermath of the 2015 Nepal earthquake, Cher supported organizations providing aid to affected communities.

Her humanitarian work often extends to hands-on involvement. In 2018, she made headlines for her efforts to help relocate and support refugees stranded in European detention centers. Her compassion for those displaced by war and conflict reflects a broader commitment to human rights and dignity.

Animal Welfare Advocacy

Cher's activism also extends to animal rights. She has been a vocal critic of animal cruelty and has supported numerous organizations dedicated to animal welfare. One of her most high-profile campaigns involved the rescue of

Kaavan, an elephant who had been kept in deplorable conditions in a Pakistani zoo. After learning about Kaavan's plight, Cher launched a global campaign to secure his release. In 2020, after years of advocacy, Kaavan was finally relocated to a sanctuary in Cambodia. Cher's efforts were documented in the film *Cher & the Loneliest Elephant*, which highlighted both her dedication and the broader issue of animal welfare.

Political Activism: Fearless and Outspoken

Cher's political activism is as bold and unfiltered as her personality. She has never shied away from expressing her views, often using her platform to challenge political leaders and advocate for social justice. Her political involvement spans decades, reflecting a deep commitment to issues ranging from civil rights and healthcare to environmental protection.

A Vocal Critic and Advocate

Throughout her career, Cher has been a vocal critic of policies and leaders she believes perpetuate injustice. Her social media presence, particularly on platforms like Twitter, has become a battleground for her political activism. She has consistently spoken out against policies she views as harmful, particularly those affecting marginalized communities.

Cher's activism is not limited to criticism; she has also been actively involved in promoting voter engagement and education. She has participated in numerous campaigns encouraging people to vote, particularly focusing on young and disenfranchised voters. Her message is clear: democracy is a responsibility, and every voice matters.

Philanthropy: Giving Back

Cher's philanthropic efforts are extensive, reflecting a genuine desire to give back. She has supported numerous charities over the years, ranging from children's hospitals and cancer research organizations to educational initiatives and veterans' support groups. Her philanthropy is often quiet and understated, driven by a sense of duty rather than a desire for recognition.

In 2016, Cher partnered with Icelandic Glacial to donate over 180,000 bottles of water to Flint, Michigan, during the city's water crisis. Her contribution was more than just a donation; it was a call to action, highlighting the systemic failures that had led to the crisis.

Legacy of Activism

Cher's activism and philanthropy are integral to her legacy. She is more than an entertainer; she is a force for change, a voice for the voiceless, and a beacon of resilience and compassion. Her journey reflects a deep belief in the power of individual action and the importance of standing up for what is right.

In a world where fame is often fleeting and superficial, Cher's commitment to activism and philanthropy sets her apart. She has used her platform not just to entertain but to educate, inspire, and provoke change. Her impact extends far beyond the stage, leaving an indelible mark on the world.

Chapter 9

Living Legend

Cher's journey has spanned more than six decades, and as she looks back on her storied career, one undeniable truth stands out: she has become a living legend. Her path to superstardom, shaped by talent, resilience, and an unrelenting drive to push boundaries, has been marked by numerous milestones, awards, and honors that cement her place as one of the most iconic figures in entertainment history. From receiving lifetime achievement awards to making history as an inductee into the Rock and Roll Hall of Fame, Cher's legacy is a testament to her enduring influence and unparalleled success. This chapter reflects on these monumental moments in her career and the recognition she has earned worldwide.

Lifetime Achievements: A Career of Firsts and Forever

Cher's career is a mosaic of groundbreaking accomplishments, and she has been recognized with numerous accolades that honor not just her artistry but her cultural significance. It's not simply the awards she has collected, but the sheer breadth and depth of her influence that make her stand out as a true legend.

Her first Grammy Award in 1971 for *Best New Artist* was just the beginning. Through the years, Cher has received multiple Grammy Awards, including honors for her iconic hit *Believe*, which forever changed the pop landscape with its use of auto-tune. Her role as a vocal trailblazer in music is not just about commercial success but about redefining genres and setting trends that others have followed.

In addition to the Grammy Awards, Cher has received several prestigious honors in recognition of her contributions to the entertainment industry. She was awarded the *César Award for Best Supporting Actress* in 1983 for her performance in *The Witches of Eastwick*, and in 1988, she won an *Academy Award for Best Actress* for her role in *Moonstruck*. These milestones are a reflection of the versatility that has defined her career. Cher is not just a singer or an actress; she is an artist who refuses to be pigeonholed.

Her *Emmy* wins, *Golden Globes*, and *People's Choice Awards* further solidify her place in history as a true legend. Each honor represents a moment in time where Cher broke new ground, captivated audiences, and set the stage for others to follow. These accolades are a testament not just to her talent but to her cultural significance as an icon of modern entertainment.

Rock and Roll Hall of Fame: Induction Into Immortality

In 1998, Cher achieved a major milestone that placed her in the annals of music history forever: her induction into the Rock and Roll Hall of Fame. This recognition was not just a personal victory but a momentous occasion for her fans, the music community, and the pop culture landscape.

The induction was a long-awaited honor, given Cher's groundbreaking contributions to music and her ability to transcend genres. Her induction was made all the more special by the fact that she was inducted alongside her former partner and musical collaborator, Sonny Bono. The two had redefined the pop music scene in the 1960s, with hits like *I Got You Babe* becoming instant anthems of youth culture.

The ceremony was a celebration of her legacy, with tributes from fellow artists and industry veterans who spoke to her influence and enduring popularity. As she took the stage, Cher embodied the essence of a living legend, a figure whose impact on the music world had spanned decades and would continue to resonate for generations to come. Her speech was a reflection of her journey—humble yet powerful, acknowledging the struggles and triumphs that led her to that moment.

Cher's induction into the Rock and Roll Hall of Fame cemented her place alongside the greatest musicians in history. She joined the ranks of artists like Elvis Presley, The Beatles, and Aretha Franklin—legends whose music has defined the fabric of popular culture. For Cher, this recognition was not just about her musical legacy but also about the countless lives she had touched through her work.

Global Recognition: A Worldwide Icon

Cher's influence transcends borders, and her recognition is global. While she may have started her career in the United States, her impact has been felt around the world, from Europe to Asia to South America. Cher's music has become a universal language, resonating with fans from all walks of life, regardless of nationality or language.

Her worldwide recognition can be traced to her ability to connect with people through her authenticity. She has never been afraid to be unapologetically herself, whether it was through her eclectic fashion choices, her defiant stance against social norms, or her raw, emotional performances. Her music, with its infectious melodies and deeply personal lyrics, resonates with listeners who find solace in her vulnerability and strength.

International Tours and Cultural Significance

Cher's global tours, particularly the *Farewell Tour* in 2002, have been monumental in showcasing her worldwide appeal. The *Farewell Tour* was initially supposed to be her last, but its massive success led to the creation of additional tours and residencies. It solidified her as a global force, capable of filling arenas and stadiums around the world, and it showcased her ability to blend music with performance art in ways few entertainers ever have.

Through her international tours, Cher has connected with fans in every corner of the globe. In places like Australia, where her concerts sell out within hours, or in Europe, where her music remains a staple on the airwaves, Cher is celebrated not just as an entertainer but as a cultural ambassador of empowerment. She continues to inspire generations with her messages of self-acceptance, individuality, and resilience.

A Symbol of Longevity: Reinventing Success Across Decades

Cher's ability to remain relevant over such a long period of time is one of the most striking aspects of her career. In a world that often favors the fleeting over the enduring, Cher has consistently reinvented herself and her art, ensuring her place in the spotlight despite the passing years.

This longevity is perhaps most evident in her ongoing cultural relevance. Cher remains a beloved figure in pop culture, often referenced in memes, TV shows, and social media. Her quotes, style, and songs continue to resonate with new generations of fans who discover her music long after its initial release. Cher's career is a testament to the power of reinvention, but it is also proof that true legends never fade—they evolve.

Cher's public image, constantly evolving but always rooted in authenticity, is what has made her a timeless figure. From her early days as the *Goddess of Pop* to her role as a fearless advocate for LGBTQ+ rights, her journey is one of personal growth, resilience, and unmatched creativity.

Reflection on Legacy: A True Living Legend

Today, as Cher reflects on her decades-long career, she finds herself more than just an entertainer. She is a global symbol of strength, empowerment, and reinvention. She is a living legend, not defined by any one moment or achievement but by her lifelong dedication to breaking barriers, challenging conventions, and inspiring others to follow their own paths.

Cher has often said that she is just as surprised as anyone by her continued relevance, but that humility only adds to her appeal. Her journey, from a small-town girl to one of the most celebrated figures in entertainment history, is proof that with passion, authenticity, and the courage to change, one can truly create a legacy that lasts beyond a lifetime.

Cher's story is far from over, but as she continues to break new ground, one thing is certain: the world will continue to recognize her as a true living legend.

Chapter 10

Legacy in 2024 and Beyond

Cher's legacy is not just defined by the music she made, the movies she starred in, or the incredible number of awards she has won; it is also shaped by the lives she has touched, the boundaries she has pushed, and the future she continues to influence. As we stand in 2024, Cher remains an icon whose impact on the cultural, social, and entertainment landscapes is as strong as ever. This chapter explores how Cher's legacy is evolving, the ways she continues to inspire new generations of artists, thinkers, and dreamers, and the long-lasting mark she will leave on the world.

A Blueprint for Reinvention: Inspiring the Next Generation of Artists

Cher's most enduring trait is her ability to reinvent herself while staying true to her core essence. She is the epitome of evolution in the entertainment industry—constantly shifting genres, sounds, and images while remaining relevant and influential. In 2024, this legacy of reinvention continues to inspire young artists who are navigating a rapidly changing digital and cultural landscape.

Her role as a trailblazer in the pop and entertainment industry has created a roadmap for aspiring musicians, actors, and performers who seek to carve their own paths. Today's artists, especially in the realms of pop and music production, look up to Cher as a symbol of self-expression and reinvention. The music industry is no longer just about maintaining one sound or image; it's about adaptability, artistic freedom, and creating a personal connection with the audience—values that Cher has embodied throughout her career.

Cher's influence can be seen in a number of young, emerging artists who are not afraid to mix genres, experiment with technology, and use their platform for activism. From pop stars like Lady Gaga to rock innovators like St. Vincent, the blueprint Cher created for blending the commercial with the avant-garde has influenced a wide range of talent. Her use of fashion, bold statements, and experimental sounds has encouraged new artists to express themselves without fear of judgment or limitations.

One example is the widespread use of auto-tune, popularized in part by Cher's 1998 hit *Believe*. What was once considered a purely electronic trick in music production became a hallmark of modern pop and electronic music, adopted by artists across genres. Cher's fearlessness in experimenting with sound and technology has made her a pioneering figure whose impact stretches far beyond her own discography.

Cher in the Digital Age: A Social Media Queen

Cher's relevance in the digital age is a testament to her ability to adapt and thrive in new environments. While many icons from her era have struggled to transition into the social media-driven world of today, Cher has embraced platforms like Twitter, Instagram, and TikTok, maintaining her connection to fans and remaining a cultural force.

Cher has over 3 million followers on Twitter and nearly 6 million on Instagram, where she posts everything from personal reflections to politically charged messages. Her Twitter account is a dynamic mix of humor, activism, and occasional memes, which keeps her deeply connected with both longtime fans and a younger audience that grew up in a digital world. She has mastered the art of staying relevant in the age of social media, with her sharp wit and authenticity resonating with audiences across the globe.

Cher's involvement in social media isn't just about self-promotion; it's about using her platform for activism. Whether it's speaking out for women's rights, LGBTQ+ rights, or political causes close to her heart, Cher uses her social media presence to raise awareness and mobilize her followers for social change. In many ways, her Twitter feed has become an extension of her activist work, bridging the gap between her status as an entertainer and her role as a vocal advocate for causes she believes in.

What's more, Cher has found a unique way to connect with younger generations who might not have grown up with her music but still identify with her bold, unconventional spirit. Her legacy is now being shared, reinterpreted, and reimagined by millennials and Gen Z, creating a digital echo that further solidifies her cultural importance.

Activism Beyond the Spotlight: Cher's Lasting Impact on Social Change

While Cher is often celebrated for her groundbreaking work in music and film, her activism has also had a profound impact on the world, especially in the areas of LGBTQ+ rights, women's empowerment, and humanitarian causes. As we move deeper into the 21st century, Cher's advocacy work continues to influence social movements and inspire others to use their platforms for meaningful change.

Cher has been a staunch advocate for the LGBTQ+ community for decades. Her work, both in front of the camera and behind the scenes, has helped raise awareness and challenge societal norms. From her role in *The Sonny & Cher Comedy Hour*, where she broke barriers with her progressive attitudes toward gender and sexuality, to her support for LGBTQ+ rights throughout her career, Cher has consistently been a voice for marginalized communities.

In recent years, Cher's activism has only intensified. She founded the *Cher Charitable Foundation* in 1988, focusing on causes such as children's rights, homelessness, and fighting AIDS. She has consistently used her influence to draw attention to important issues. Cher's tireless work as an advocate has inspired countless others to stand up for justice, equality, and human rights, showing that the fight for social change is far from over.

Her outspoken stance on political issues, particularly in the United States, also remains a key part of her legacy. Cher has never shied away from using her platform to address topics ranging from healthcare to climate change, often using social media as a vehicle to engage her followers in activism. Whether she's speaking about the importance of voting, the challenges of poverty, or her passion for protecting the environment, Cher's commitment to activism serves as a powerful example of how entertainment figures can use their influence for positive societal impact.

Cher's Influence in the Arts and Culture: Shaping the Future

Cher's legacy is woven deeply into the fabric of popular culture. She is referenced in movies, television shows, books, and even in academic circles, where scholars analyze her work as an example of an artist who transcended the limits of her time. Her career has been the subject of countless discussions on cultural theory, identity politics, and the representation of women in entertainment.

Her iconic fashion, distinctive voice, and groundbreaking performances have made her an ongoing muse for artists, filmmakers, and designers. In 2024, Cher continues to shape the future of fashion and entertainment. The *Cher look*—from her extravagant costumes in the 1960s and 1970s to her daring red carpet moments today—remains an enduring influence on designers and stylists alike. The blend of avant-garde style with pop sensibilities has kept Cher a relevant figure in the world of fashion, with her ability to make bold statements and set trends continuing to resonate.

Even in film, Cher's influence can be seen in the performances of contemporary actors who cite her as an inspiration. Her ability to balance comedy and drama, as well as her fearless portrayals of strong female characters, continues to inspire actors who want to carve out their own paths in Hollywood.

Conclusion: Cher's Legacy—Eternal and Ever-Evolving

As Cher's journey continues into the future, one thing is certain: her legacy will never fade. Her influence on music, film, fashion, activism, and culture is timeless. With each passing year, her impact continues to grow, touching new generations of artists, thinkers, and dreamers.

Cher has shown the world that reinvention is not just a tool for surviving the entertainment industry, but a way to thrive and leave an indelible mark on society. In 2024 and beyond, Cher will remain a symbol of boldness, resilience, and creativity. She will continue to inspire those who dare to dream big and be unapologetically themselves. Cher's legacy is not one confined to the past; it is one that will echo for generations to come.

Epilogue

The Music Never Ends

As the final notes of a song echo into silence, and the lights of the stage slowly fade, Cher reflects on a career that has spanned decades, defied norms, and inspired millions across the globe. Her journey—one of relentless reinvention, artistic bravery, and deep connection with her fans—has brought her to this moment, a place where she can look back on her extraordinary life and feel a profound sense of gratitude. But even as she takes a pause, the music continues to play, and her message to her fans, her legacy, and her thoughts on the future of fame, art, and life are as clear and passionate as ever.

A Message to Her Fans: A Legacy of Love and Gratitude

Cher's relationship with her fans is not just that of an entertainer to an audience; it is a bond forged through shared experiences, mutual respect, and unwavering love. Through her music, her films, and her activism, she has connected with millions of people, giving them a sense of belonging, strength, and hope. In

her eyes, they are more than just followers—
they are family.

As she reflects on the people who have
supported her throughout her career, Cher
offers a heartfelt message of thanks to the
fans who have stayed by her side through
every reinvention, every high, and every low.
"The music never ends, and neither does my
love for you," she says. "I am who I am
because of you, and I will always be grateful
for the way you've embraced me, supported
me, and let me be part of your lives."

For Cher, the relationship with her fans is
symbiotic. Their energy has fueled her career
and inspired her to continue pushing the limits
of what is possible, even after all these years.
Whether it's through social media interactions,
live performances, or simply sharing her story,
Cher remains deeply committed to her
fanbase, feeling as though their stories are
intertwined with her own.

On the Future of Fame: Evolving in the Digital Age

As a star who achieved fame long before the
digital age reshaped the entertainment
industry, Cher has witnessed firsthand the
transformation of fame—from the days of TV

interviews and tabloids to the era of social media and streaming platforms. Fame, she believes, has evolved in ways both empowering and challenging, especially for the younger generation of artists who are navigating a vastly different world than the one she entered in the 1960s.

"In some ways, fame today is more accessible," Cher muses. "Anyone with a phone and a dream can find a platform to be heard. But in other ways, it's harder. The pressure is constant. The scrutiny is relentless. There's no real privacy anymore. Fame has become a 24/7 cycle."

Yet, Cher has always believed in the power of authenticity—whether it's in her own career or in the world of fame at large. "The trick is to stay true to yourself," she advises. "It's easy to get lost in the noise, but you have to remember who you are, what you stand for, and why you started in the first place."

She acknowledges the ways social media has democratized fame, giving new artists more opportunities than ever to build careers and reach audiences without relying on traditional gatekeepers. However, she also highlights the challenges that come with the pressures of instant visibility and public opinion.

But Cher remains optimistic. "There's room for everyone," she says, reflecting on the changing dynamics of fame. "The future of fame will be about personal connection—how you resonate with people. It's less about being seen everywhere and more about how you make them feel. And that's something that will never go out of style."

On the Future of Art: The Freedom to Create

Cher's evolution as an artist has been defined by her fearless approach to experimenting with new sounds, styles, and technologies. From the early days of *I Got You Babe* to the electronic revolution of *Believe*, Cher has never been afraid to push the boundaries of music and performance. And she believes the future of art will continue to be shaped by this freedom to create and innovate.

"I've always believed that art should challenge the status quo," Cher reflects. "It should make people think, feel, and, most of all, question. The future of art, in whatever form it takes, will be about breaking down walls—whether it's between genres, generations, or cultures."

Cher also sees technology playing an ever-growing role in the future of art. In a world where AI, virtual reality, and digital platforms are transforming the way music is made, performed, and consumed, Cher recognizes the potential for artists to create in ways never before imagined. But she also stresses the importance of retaining the human element in art. "Technology will never replace the heart and soul of music," she says. "It can enhance it, but at the end of the day, it's the human touch that makes art resonate."

On the Future of Life: Living Authentically, Fearlessly

As she looks ahead, Cher also reflects on the future of life itself. For someone who has defied conventional expectations in almost every aspect of her career, she has come to value authenticity and fearlessness above all else. "I've learned that life is about living on your own terms, not conforming to anyone else's idea of who you should be," she says.

Her advice to those coming after her is simple yet powerful: "Be true to yourself. Don't let the world tell you who to be. Embrace your flaws. Embrace your uniqueness. And keep going, no matter what."

Cher also encourages others to continue embracing change and growth. "Don't be afraid to reinvent yourself. You're never too old to try something new. I've done it over and over again, and it's always been worth it."

In her final words, Cher leaves us with the same hope and resilience that have defined her life and career. "Life is a journey," she concludes, "and as long as the music keeps playing, so do we. The show never ends. The music never ends. And neither does the love."

As the last echoes of her voice fade into the horizon, it is clear that Cher's journey is far from over. Her impact is eternal, her spirit unyielding, and her legacy will continue to inspire generations to come. The music, indeed, never ends.

Made in the USA
Monee, IL
17 December 2024

74199138R00046